TOP DOGS

Miniature Schnauzer

Charles and Linda George

Created by Q2AMedia
www.q2amedia.com
Editor Jeff O' Hare
Publishing Director Chester Fisher
Client Service Manager Santosh Vasudevan
Project Manager Kunal Mehrotra
Art Director Harleen Mehta
Designer Deepika Verma
Picture Researcher Nivisha Sinha

Library of Congress Cataloging-in-Publication Data
George, Charles, 1949-
Miniature schnauzer / [Charles George, Linda George].
p. cm. — (Top dogs)
Includes index.
ISBN 0-531-24934-4/978-0-531-24934-5 (pbk.)
1. Miniature schnauzer—Juvenile literature. I. George, Linda. II. Title.
SF429.M58G46 2010
636.755—dc22

Printed and bound in Heshan, China
232754 10/10
10 9 8 7 6 5 4 3 2 1

Picture Credits
t= top, b= bottom, c= center, r= right, l= left

Cover Page: Katie Little/Istockphoto, Y Tea/Shutterstock.

Title Page: Heidi Mosteller/Istockphoto.

4-5: Waldemar Dabrowski/Shutterstock; 5: Olinchuk/Shutterstock; 6-7: Hanquan Chen/Istockphoto; 7: Masterfile Corporation; 8: ImageShop/Corbis; 9: Raycan/Dreamstime; 10-11: Fotosearch/Photolibrary; 11: Volker Hopf/Shutterstock; 12-13: Aflo Aflo/Photolibrary; 13: Raycan/Dreamstime; 14: Ellinor Hall/Photolibrary; 15: Elliot Westacott/Shutterstock, Aaron Amat/Shutterstock, Yegorius/Shutterstock; 16-17: A.Van Kampen/www.dogimages.org.uk; 17: Gina Callaway/Shutterstock; 18-19: Mike Hollist/Daily Mail/Rex Features; 20: Alessandro Treguer/Dreamstime; 21: David Selby/Istockphoto; 22: Juniors Bildarchiv/Photolibrary; 23: Raywoo/Dreamstime; 24: Raywoo/Dreamstime; 25: Elliot Westacott/Shutterstock, CarlaVanWagoner/Shutterstock; 26-27: Han Thon Lim/Dreamstime; 27: Chin Kit Sen/Shutterstock; 28: Deanna Quinton Larson/Istockphoto; 29: Sgcallaway/Fotolia; 30-31: David Pearson/Rex Features; 31: Sgcallaway/Dreamstime.

Contents

What are Miniature Schnauzers?

Fast Fact

They weren't called schnauzers until the 1800s. Schnauzer means "**muzzle**" in German.

Schnauzers (*sh-now-zurz*) were first raised in Germany in the 1400s. Full-sized Schnauzers were used as herding dogs and watchdogs. **Miniature** Schnauzers were developed in the late 1800s. They were used as ratters.

Mini Schnauzers are smaller than other Schnauzers. They first came to the U.S. in 1924. Today, they are known as a type of **terrier**. They make good family pets.

North Sea

Denmark

Baltic Sea

Hamburg ● ●Schwerin

Bremen ●

Poland

Potsdam ● Berlin

Netherlands

Hannover ●

●Magdeburg

Germany

Belgium

Düsseldorf ●

●Weimar

Dresden ●

Czech Republic

Wiesbaden ● ●Mainz

Luxembourg

Saarbrücken ●

●Stuttgart

France

Switzerland

Everyone Loves Mini Schnauzers

Mini Schnauzers make great house dogs. They want to be in the middle of whatever their family is doing. They like to learn new things. They bark a lot when they are playing.

Fast Fact

Mini Schnauzers don't like strangers, but they make friends quickly.

Mini Schnauzers can be stubborn. They need to learn how to behave. Schnauzers are easier to **train** when they are young. They like doing things over and over. They also like getting a treat or a pat on the head.

Fast Fact

Mini Schnauzers need a long walk on a **leash** every day.

Mini Schnauzers Love Kids!

Mini Schnauzers will like one person more than other people. They stay with that one person most of the time. When that person is not around, they will play with someone else.

Fast Fact

Mini Schnauzers are usually good with children. They bark when someone they don't know comes near.

Schnauzers love playing outside and getting exercise. They love to run and play with children. When they use up their energy, they need a nap.

Fast Fact

Mini Schnauzers move quickly. They are tough little dogs.

Puppy Love!

Most **litters** of Mini Schnauzers have 4 or 5 puppies. Their eyes won't open for about a week. For the first six weeks, they will sleep a lot. Keep them in a warm, dry place.

Fast Fact

Never try to open a puppy's eyes too soon. That could blind the puppy.

Mini Schnauzers weigh 4 to 9 ounces (0.1-0.25 kg) at birth. They are a little smaller than a can of soda. They weigh about half as much as a can of soda. You should hold them gently because they are so small.

Fast Fact

Mini Schnauzers get more active as they grow. They grow fast!

Choosing a Mini Schnauzer Puppy

When you choose your Mini Schnauzer puppy, watch the litter first. Choose a puppy that plays a lot with the others. It will play well with you, too.

Fast Fact

Meet your puppy's mom and dad, if you can. If its parents are nice dogs, the puppy will be, too.

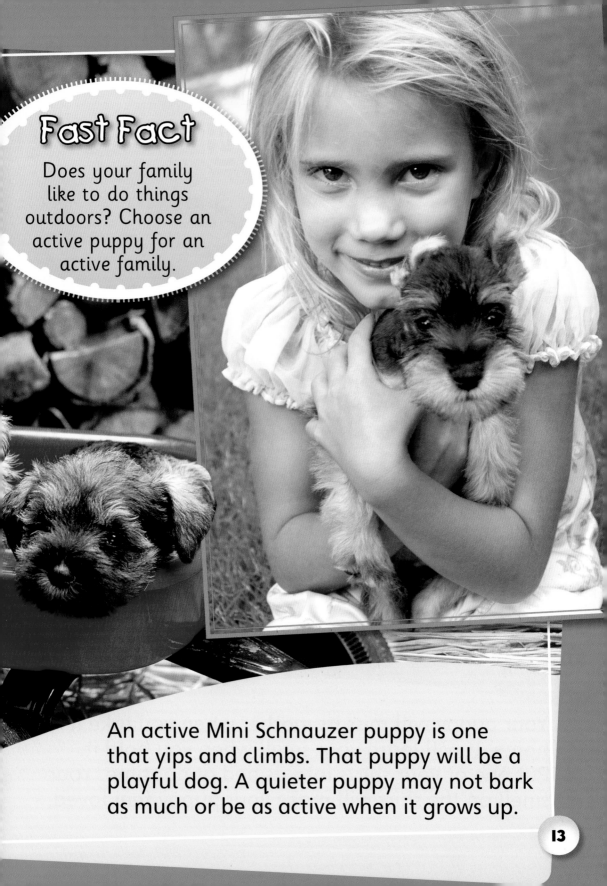

Does your family like to do things outdoors? Choose an active puppy for an active family.

An active Mini Schnauzer puppy is one that yips and climbs. That puppy will be a playful dog. A quieter puppy may not bark as much or be as active when it grows up.

Taking Care of Your Puppy

Fast Fact

Let your Mini Schnauzer meet other people and animals.

Your puppy will miss its mother when you take it home. It will learn your smell when you hold it. Put one of your shirts into its bed at naptime. Your smell on the shirt will make your puppy feel loved.

Give your Mini Schnauzer toys to play with and to chew. A puppy likes to sleep with its toys. Your puppy will often feel hungry or thirsty. Give it puppy food and clean, cool water.

Fast Fact

Give your puppy treats only when you are training it. You don't want your puppy to gain too much weight.

How Big Do Mini Schnauzers Get?

Mini Schnauzers weigh about 13-18 pounds (5.9-8.2 kg) when they grow up. They stand 12-14 inches (30.5-35.6 cm) tall. Mini Schnauzers are small dogs. They are easy to take on car trips.

Fast Fact

Mini Schnauzers love riding in the car.

Full-grown Mini Schnauzers are small enough to be lap dogs. They love cuddling with you on the couch. They also like to sleep at the foot of your bed. This is okay, since they don't **shed** their hair.

Brushing Hair and Clipping Nails

A Mini Schnauzer's hair should be brushed every day. This keeps the hair from getting tangled. A Mini Schnauzer should be taken to a **groomer** at least twice a year. A groomer will give your dog a bath and trim its nails.

Fast Fact

A Mini Schnauzer's outer coat feels tough and **wiry**, but it also has softer hair underneath.

A Mini Schnauzer doesn't shed a lot of hair. A Mini Schnauzer may be a good choice for people with **allergies**. If dog hair makes you sneeze, a Mini Schnauzer might be just right for you.

Fast Fact

Mini Schnauzers come in different colors.

A Fun Dog

Mini Schnauzers have lots of energy. They like to be part of family activities. They love being watched by everyone. They may do crazy things to get you to watch them.

Fast Fact

Mini Schnauzers can be real clowns. They will make you laugh!

Fast Fact

Some Mini Schnauzers wipe their mouths on furniture. This can leave a dark streak where their mouths have been.

Your Mini Schnauzer does funny things. It has a fuzzy mouth. It gets food and water on its face. When it wipes its face on the carpet, it looks very silly.

Make Room for Your Schnauzer!

Because Mini Schnauzers are small, they fit nicely into any size house. They can run around inside or in a fenced backyard. They like to go walking on a leash, wearing a **harness**.

Fast Fact

Harnesses are better for your dog than **collars**. A collar can choke when the dog pulls too hard on the leash.

Fast Fact

Larger Schnauzers are used on farms. They help herd cattle. They are also used as guard dogs.

There are two other sizes of Schnauzers other than Mini Schnauzers. A regular Schnauzer can weigh 35-45 pounds (15.9-20.4 kg). A Giant Schnauzer can weigh as much as 90 pounds (40.8 kg).

So Smart!

A Mini Schnauzer is a smart dog. Train your dog when it is young. Teach it manners. Sometimes, it won't do what you tell it. Teach it to do what you say.

You have to teach your Mini Schnauzer that you are the boss. Once they learn that they have to do what you say, they are happy to obey.

Fast Fact

Schnauzers may chase and kill small animals if you don't watch them!

Frisky Dogs

A Mini Schnauzer may get bored when it's left alone. It could get into trouble! Leave toys with your dog when you aren't there to play with it. If it doesn't have toys, it might chew on your shoes!

Fast Fact

Mini Schnauzers like being around people. They get sad if left alone too long.

Mini Schnauzers try to keep their people safe from strangers. They bark at animals they don't know. Let them get to know other people and animals slowly. They may growl at other dogs. This is their way of talking to them.

Fast Fact

Mini Schnauzers make a strange howling sound when they don't want to do as they've been told.

Mini Schnauzers Helping People

A Mini Schnauzer is a great family pet. People who live alone like having a Mini Schnauzer for a pet. The dog keeps them from being lonely.

Fast Fact

When a Mini Schnauzer barks, it may sound like a much bigger dog.

Some Mini Schnauzers are **therapy dogs**. Therapy dogs visit people who are sick or who live alone. Mini Schnauzers are friendly dogs. This makes them ideal therapy dogs.

Fast Fact

Being petted is good for the dog, and good for people, too.

Best of the Breed

Mini Schnauzers are mostly family pets. Some are entered in dog shows, like the Westminster Kennel Club Dog Show. This show is held each February at Madison Square Garden in New York City.

Fast Fact

The Westminster Dog Show has been held every year for the past 134 years!